To Jacob
G.A.

To Caroline,
with thanks for everything
D.W.

Other books by Giles Andreae
and David Wojtowycz

Rumble in the Jungle
Commotion in the Ocean
The Lion Who Wanted to Love

LITTLE TIGER PRESS
N16 W23390 Stoneridge Drive, Waukesha, WI 53188
First published in the United States 2000
Originally published in Great Britain 1999 by
Orchard Books, London
• CIP Data is available
First American Edition • ISBN 1-888444-75-4
Printed in Belgium
1 3 5 7 9 10 8 6 4 2

Cock-a-doodle-doo! Barnyard Hullabaloo

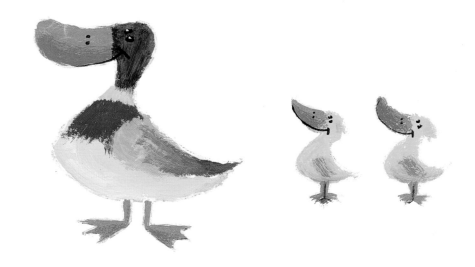

Giles Andreae

Illustrated by

David Wojtowycz

LITTLE TIGER PRESS

Early in the morning
As the sun begins to rise,
The pigs are feeling hungry
And they're snorting in their sties.

The rooster wakes the farm up
With a cock-a-doodle-doo!
The sheepdog won't stop barking,
And the cows begin to moo.

There's a stomping in the stables
And there's bleating in the barn,
So let's climb aboard the tractor
And explore this noisy farm.

Rooster

Cock-a-doodle-doo!
Cock-a-doodle-doo!
I'm the rockin' rooster, baby,
Tell me, who are you?

Chickens

We chickens are covered with feathers
All over our wings and our legs,
So of course we could fly
If we wanted to try
But we're too busy laying these eggs.

Cow

Sometimes I moo while I'm chewing
I hope you don't think that it's rude,
But mooing and chewing
Are what I like doing.
Do you moo when you chew your food?

moooooo!

Sheepdog

I am the farmer's old sheepdog,
His faithful and loyal best friend.
I've been by his side from the day I was born
And I'll stay with him right to the end.

Barnyard Cat

Hello, I'm the big barnyard kitty
I sleep in the shade of the house
But I always keep one eye half open
To spot every passing plump mouse.

yikes!

Pigs

I love taking care of my piglets
And watching them wriggle and squeal.
They clamber all over each other all day
To snuffle around for a meal.

wriggle
wriggle

Donkey

It's wonderful being a donkey,
I simply spend hours and hours
Just wandering around
On the soft grassy ground
Sniffing the sweet-smelling flowers.

Turkey

I've got these funny, floppy things
That hang down from my neck,
They dangle when I gobble
And they wobble when I peck.

gobble

gobble

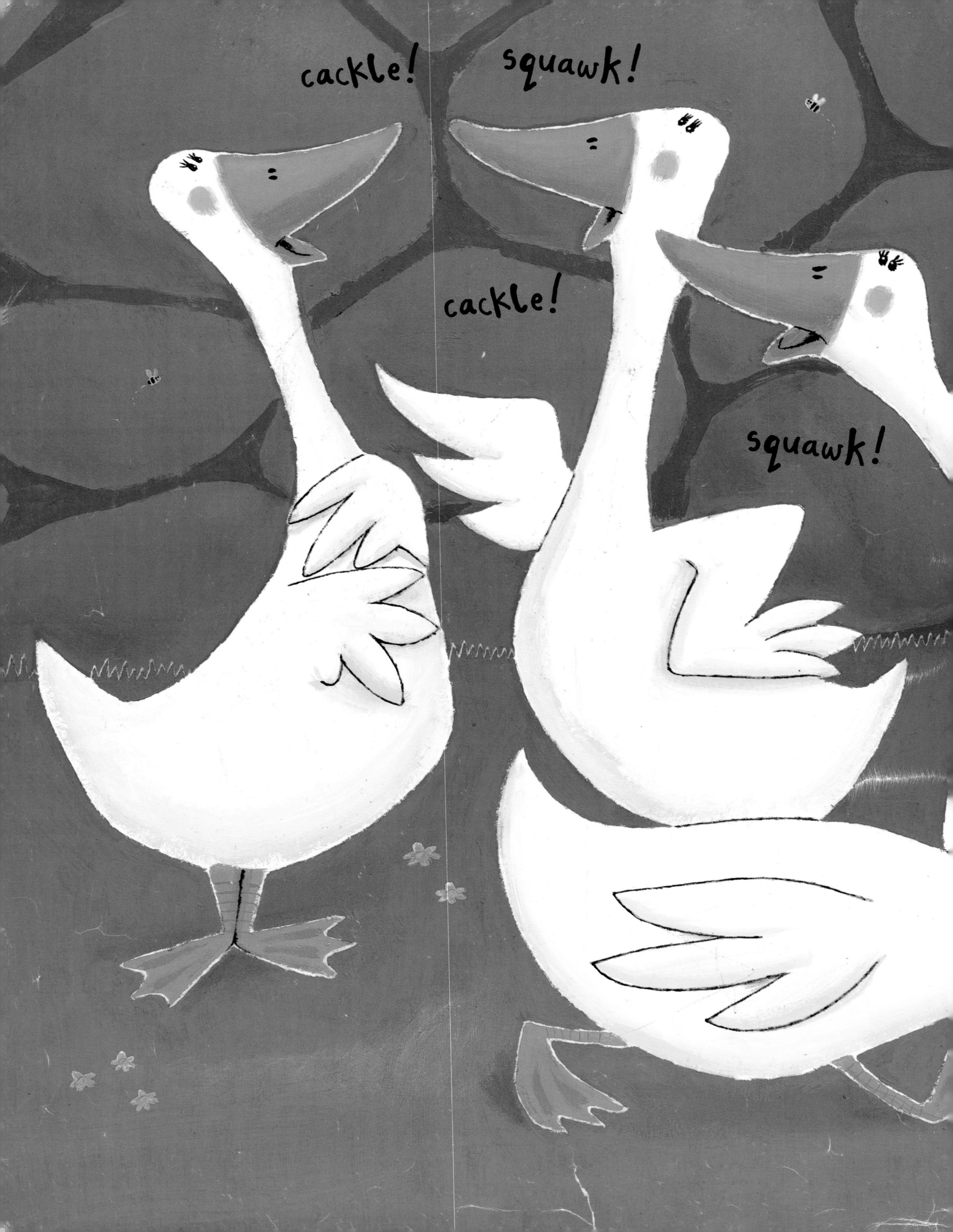
cackle!
squawk!
cackle!
squawk!

Geese

We waddle about in the barnyard
And make so much noise when we talk
That wandering goslings rush out of our way
As we babble and cackle and squawk.

cackle!

skip   skip

Sheep

I've got gorgeous fluffy fleece
Which makes me very proud,
So I skip around my meadow
Make-believing I'm a cloud.

Goat

I sometimes hang out by the sheep-pen
Chuckling into my beard.
Sheep often think that they're better than us
But goats never need to get sheared!

chuckle!
chuckle!

clippety clop !

Horse

There's nothing like hay when you're hungry,
I'm happy to munch a whole bale,
But sometimes I stop
For a clippety-clop
Or to flick a few flies with my tail.

Bull

I love to snort steam from my nostrils,
It makes me look angry and tough,
And then I start scraping my hoof on the ground
If that isn't scary enough.

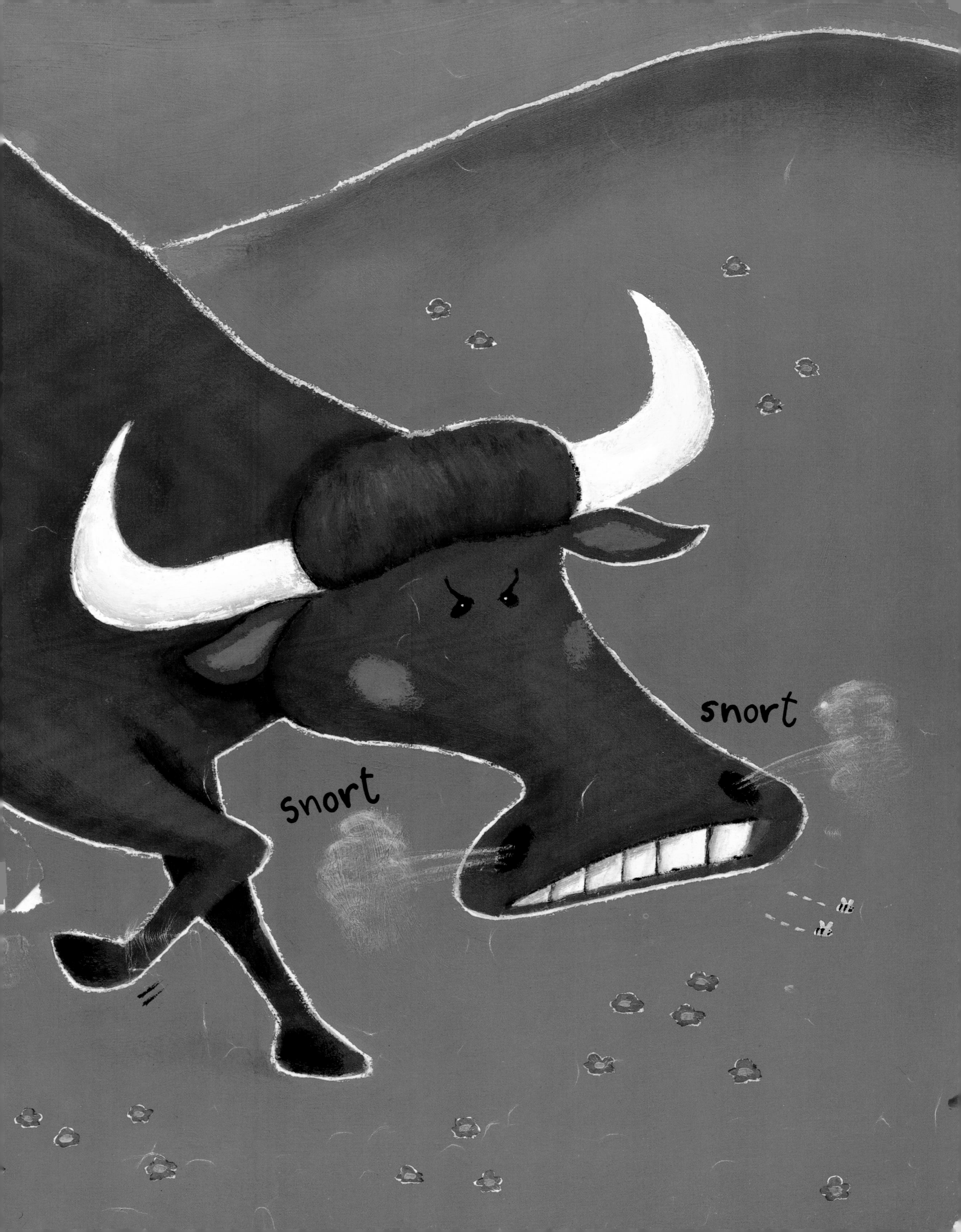
snort
snort

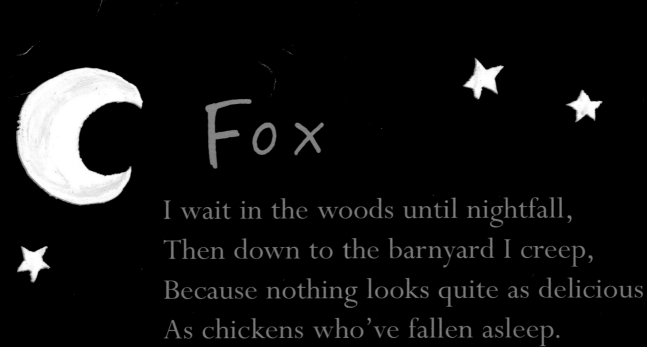

Fox

I wait in the woods until nightfall,
Then down to the barnyard I creep,
Because nothing looks quite as delicious
As chickens who've fallen asleep.

Owl

I always hunt at nighttime
And I sleep throughout the day.
"Ter-wit, ter-woo," you'll hear me cry,
Out searching for my prey.

*ter-wit
ter-woo*

Now it's nighttime in the barnyard
And the moon is shining bright,
It's time to leave the animals
And wave them all goodnight.

The cows are feeling sleepy
So they settle on the ground,
It won't be very long now
Till they're sleeping safe and sound.

The horse is in his stable
And the hens are in their shed,
But the sheepdog's fallen fast asleep
Inside the farmer's bed!